THE JUNIOR THUNDER LORD

BY LAURENCE YEP ◆◆ PICTURES BY ROBERT VAN NUTT

HOUGHTON MIFFLIN   BOSTON • MORRIS PLAINS, NJ

California • Colorado • Georgia • Illinois • New Jersey • Texas

Designed by Leslie Bauman.

The Junior Thunder Lord, by Laurence Yep, illustrated by Robert Van Nutt. Text copyright © 1994 by Lawrence Yep. Illustrations copyright © 1994 by Robert Van Nutt. The text is reprinted by arrangement with Curtis Brown, Ltd., on behalf of the Author. The illustrations are reprinted by arrangement with the publishers, Troll Communications LLC.

Houghton Mifflin Edition, 2001

Printed in the U. S. A.

ISBN: 0-618-06264-5

123456789-B-06 05 04 03 02 01 00

To Joanne, who told me to write this story.
LY

For my wife, Julia, my traveling companion to
the four corners of the imagination.
RVN

Once there was a boy named Yue who had trouble learning his lessons. His teacher would get so mad that he would beat Yue. But the smartest boy, Xia, felt sorry for him. "Those at the top," Xia said, "should help those at the bottom."

Yue never forgot those words, even when he grew up and became a merchant. He was always helping his neighbors.

However, there came a time when the rains did not fall for three years in a row. The crops died in the fields so nobody had anything to trade. Yue had to go south to find customers for his goods. He bid farewell to his family.

After traveling through many places, Yue eventually reached a strange peninsula called Thunder County, where the sea boomed and crashed against the land. In town, he found a crowd hauling a cart with drums joined to one another. The drummers raised a din loud enough to drown out the noise of the surf.

Squeezing his way through the jammed streets, he sat down at an inn and asked the innkeeper what was going on. "Today we honor the thunder lords," the innkeeper explained. "With their stone axes, they make the thunder and help the dragons bring rain. You can find stone chips wherever they fashion their axes."

Yue had no sooner asked for noodles when a big, scowling man shuffled in and plopped down on the same bench. He was so hairy that he looked like a bear squeezed into a blue leather vest and bright red trousers. Around his waist was a leopard skin sash.

"Don't worry, sir," the innkeeper whispered to Yue. "Bear Face is as stupid as he is big. He doesn't know about money or the simplest things. Don't pay any attention to him. He'll go away eventually."

"If my friend, Xia, had thought that way, I'd still be in school," Yue said. "Please bring a bowl of noodles for Bear Face as well."

When the innkeeper brought their orders, Bear Face immediately plunged a hand into his bowl and crammed noodles into his mouth.

"You're disgusting," the innkeeper scolded Bear Face. "Where are your manners? Use your chopsticks."

Bear Face ignored the innkeeper as he gulped down mouthful after mouthful. "Poor fellow, he eats that way because he's starved," Yue said. "Bring him another bowl."

The innkeeper snorted. "Don't be so nice to that slob. He won't even thank you."

Sure enough, when Bear Face finished his second bowl, he banged it on the table. "More," he demanded.

And Yue felt so sorry for Bear Face that he ordered a whole shoulder of pork and stuffed dumplings.

When Bear Face had finally gobbled up enough for six, he reached out a huge, greasy hand and yanked Yue toward him so that they were nose to nose. "I haven't had a meal like that for almost three years. In all my wanderings, you're the only one who's been kind to me."

Yue stammered. "Th-th-think nothing of it. When you're at the top, you have to help the person on the bottom."

The big man thought a moment and then belched right into Yue's face. "How true. It's written on your face that you're in mortal danger, so I'd better go with you."

That was the last thing Yue wanted, and he told Bear Face to stay. But the big, ugly fellow stuck by his promise. The rest of that day Bear Face shambled behind Yue wherever he went.

By late afternoon, Yue was sorry he had ever done the fellow a favor. When he reached the bustling docks, he turned around. "You've wasted your time," Yue said, "for I am leaving on the next boat."

"Then I sail, too," Bear Face insisted.

And sure enough, he plodded right after Yue onto the ship. The crew tried to throw him off, but when they couldn't budge the hairy giant, an embarrassed Yue paid his fare. "This is the last time I spend any money on you," Yue grumbled in exasperation.

They had no sooner left sight of the land when a storm
swept in and capsized the boat, throwing everyone into the dark
waters.

As Yue began to sink, he felt himself seized by a big fist and

set upon a hairy back. As Yue clung to his guardian's neck, Bear Face swam easily through the choppy waves to shore. When he had saved the crew and the other passengers, he paddled back out for Yue's goods.

On the beach, Yue tried to thank Bear Face, but the hairy man just waved his hand in farewell. "We're even now," he said.

Yue grabbed his arm. "Don't go. You saved my life."

The huge, hairy man was surprised. "Think of how it will look. I've already spent too much time with you."

"I don't care," Yue swore. "They can call me crazy if they want. You're my friend."

When Bear Face smiled, it was such a fierce, scary scowl that Yue would have run away if Bear Face had not recently saved his life.

The two traveled on. When Yue had sold all his goods, he and Bear Face headed home.

The closer they got to Yue's village, the worse the drought became and the angrier Bear Face grew. When they reached Yue's village, the wells were full of dust and the plants were like burned whiskers and the trees mere sticks.

"This is awful. What a botch-up!" a sweating Bear Face growled.

Yue sighed and fanned himself with his hand. "I know, but what can we do?"

"Those on top should always help those on the bottom."
Looking up at the sky, he shouted, "Come brothers. My time is
done."

Yue gave a gasp when he saw dark clouds appear on the
horizon and sweep toward them.

Bear Face held his arms out toward the clouds. "Over here,
brothers!"

The coming storm rumbled in answer. Bear Face's hands changed into paws with golden claws, and so did his feet.

"Who are you?" Yue gasped in amazement.

"I am Bear Face, a junior thunder lord," he boomed. A black stone axe appeared in Bear Face's hand, and a band of little drums was suddenly strung across his shoulders. "You mortals thought I was a fool because I didn't know your ways, but how would you fare up in my sky country?"

Yue fell to his knees. "Forgive me, lord. I did not know."

Bear Face smiled affectionately at Yue. "But I am also your friend." Then with a whoop Bear Face began to beat the drums with his axe. Peals of thunder shook the houses and rattled the roof tiles.

"What are you doing down here, lord?" Yue wondered.

"I told an uppity dragon what I thought of him," Bear Face explained. "Unfortunately, he was a king, so I was condemned to live on the earth for three years. But now my punishment is over!" Bear Face pounded his drums faster and faster. With each stroke, thunder crashed through the village. Storm clouds drew overhead.

Bear Face's leathery vest instantly changed into a pair of powerful blue wings ten feet across. "Now let me show you what it's really like to be on top."

Hugging Yue against his chest, Bear Face flapped his great wings and soared into the sky toward the dark storm clouds.

Dragons prowled the flanks of the storm while creatures
just like Bear Face drove the huge clouds along with cracks of
thunder. Dark as water buffalo, the clouds lumbered across the
sky.

As soon as the other creatures saw Bear Face, they called
out their greetings and swirled around.

"I go away for a little while and you let things slide until there's a terrible mess below," he scolded them. Then he herded one cloud to the side and said to Yue, "Push the side of the cloud, friend."

When Yue did, rain began to fall. "You can aim better than that," Bear Face hinted.

Down below the towns were the size of beans, but Yue managed to find his home. He was careful to squeeze the spongy cloud so that every drop of rain fell there.

When the cloud was gone, Bear Face regretfully said it was time for them to part. Pulling the sash from his waist, he told Yue to take hold of one end and he would lower Yue down to the village.

"Farewell, friend," Bear Face said. "When I was at my lowest, you lifted me up. I won't ever forget you." The next

moment the air whistled past Yue's ears. Suddenly he was standing right outside his home.

All around him, the streams and ponds were full, and the fields sparkled with life. As he admired the wet countryside, he heard his wife greeting him.

After that, the village always had all the rain it needed. And when it was pouring its hardest, Yue and his wife would go outside to wave up at their friend as he drove his storm clouds overhead.

This is a retelling of a story collected and published in the seventeenth century by Pu Songling in his *Liao Zhai Zhi Yi*.